Hello, Cheers!

The Art of Cheers.

Created by Jill Donohue

Hello, Cheers!

First Edition

ISBN: 979-8-3304-8862-9

For anyone inspired to paint the life they truly love. 💛

Contents

Raise Your Glass

Art & Drinks

Mix It Up

Sip & Story

Raise Your Glass

The Art of Cheers

Welcome to *Hello, Cheers!* a book that celebrates the art of connection and the moments that bring us together. You know that feeling when you're toasting with friends, whether it's Champagne or a cup of coffee? It's not just about the drink - it's about the people, the laughter, and the joy of being together. This lighthearted book is here to help you savor those moments, spark some smiles, and create new memories (and laughs). So, let's raise a glass to friendship, new experiences, and living in the moment.

Hello, Cheers! We hope every toast brings a smile...

"Let's celebrate"

"Raise your glass

"To good times"

"To new beginnings"

"Salud"

"Toast to that"

"Drink up"

"Bottoms up"

and every sip is a celebration!

"Yessss"

"Here's to me" "Here's to you" "Here's to us"

"Drink, laugh, repeat" "Woo-hoo" "We did it"

"Good vibes only"

So, raise a glass to painting the life you love! :)

Art & Drinks

Buy me
a
drink

Spicy Margarita

2 oz. tequila

1 oz. lime juice (freshly squeezed)

1/2 oz. triple sec

1/2 oz. agave syrup

2-3 slices of jalapeño

Tajín (for rimming the glass)

lime wedge or cucumber slice

In a cocktail shaker, smash jalapeño slices with lime juice. Add ingredients, ice, and shake. Pour into glass, top with lime or cucumber.

Truth or Spice?

Before each sip, everyone is asked a spicy question - something fun and lighthearted but revealing. If you don't answer, take a drink (or add an extra jalapeño slice).

Purple Rain

1½ oz. vodka

1 oz. Blue Curaçao

1 oz. grenadine

lemonade (to top)

fresh lime juice

crushed ice

lime wheel

Sip, swirl, and play some Prince to dance to.

Fill a glass with crushed ice, add ingredients, and squeeze in some fresh lime juice. Top with lemonade & lime wheel.

Play a round of "Rain or Shine" as you enjoy...

Each person shares a high point (shine) or a challenge they overcame (rain) from their week.

Espresso Martini

1½ oz. vodka

1 oz. coffee liqueur (think Kahlúa)

1 shot of freshly brewed espresso (or cold brew)

1/4 oz. simple syrup (optional for sweetness)

Fill a cocktail shaker with ice, add ingredients & shake. Strain into a chilled martini glass. Top with coffee beans or cocoa powder.

How the Story Goes...

The Espresso Martini was invented in the 1980s at Soho Brasserie (a swanky London club) for a model who asked for a drink to keep her night going. What drink have you invented? Share the story with your friends!

French Martini

2 oz. vodka

1 oz. Chambord (raspberry liqueur)

2 oz. pineapple juice

Fill a cocktail shaker with ice, add ingredients, and shake. Pour into a chilled martini glass. Top with a raspberry or lemon twist.

Fun Facts:

The French Martini was popularized in the 1980s, particularly in New York City, and inspired by the classic vodka martini with a fruity twist.

It's known for its vibrant pinkish hue, making it visually striking and popular for celebrations and special occasions.

Chardonnay

Bottle of Chardonnay

Your favorite wine glass

Best white wine! Do you agree?

Open the wine bottle, pour into your wine glass, and enjoy!

Chardonnay is a blank canvas - its flavor varies with the winemaker's touch. It can be buttery and rich to crisp and refreshing. Just like people, every Chardonnay has its own personality! :)

Guess That Flavor

Conduct a Chardonnay blind taste test with your friends - serving several types (oaked, unoaked, creamy, buttery). Then, make up a creative personality for each flavor.

Aperol Spritz

3 parts Prosecco

2 parts Aperol

1 part soda water

orange slice

Fill your glass with ice and add ingredients. Top with an orange slice.

Spritz & Compliments

The Aperol Spritz embodies Italian aperitivo culture - a time to unwind and enjoy good company. It’s about the vibe and bringing people together. Ask each person to give a sincere compliment to someone else; it's a fun way to spread positivity and joy.

Paloma Mocktail

4 oz. fresh grapefruit juice
2-4 oz. sparkling water
1/2 oz. fresh lime juice
1/2 oz. honey or simple syrup
grapefruit slice

Fill a cocktail shaker with grapefruit juice, lime juice, honey or simple syrup and shake. Add sparkling water and stir. Add a grapefruit slice for garnish.

Peaceful Paloma - Add Your Twist

The Paloma is a classic Mexican cocktail made with tequila and grapefruit soda. Its name means *dove* in Spanish, symbolizing peace. There are countless variations—if you could create your own version, what unique ingredients would you add?

KEEP IT SHAKIN'
KEEP IT SHAKIN'
KEEP IT SHAKIN'
KEEP IT SHAKIN'
KEEP IT SHAKIN'

Want to Shake Up More Drinks?

Visit www.buymeadrink.co/mixieai

Tell **Mixie AI** what cocktail you're in the mood for or what ingredients you have on hand, and it will whip up the perfect recipe in seconds.

Raise your glass to even more cocktail creativity!

Keep the party going with fresh recipes, inspiration, and virtual cheers at buymeadrink.co.

Buy Me A Drink

Mix it Up

Light, playful games to shake things up.

Would You Rather?

Would you rather sip a Piña Colada on a tropical beach or a hot spiced cider by a fireplace in a cozy lodge?

Would you rather toast with Champagne in Paris or enjoy a cold beer in a Munich beer hall?

Would you rather have a bottomless Bloody Mary brunch or unlimited sangria at a tapas bar?

Would you rather feast on tacos & margaritas or cheese & wine on a night out with friends?

Come up with your own scenarios...

This or That?

Coffee or Tea?

Lemon or Lime?

Red or White?

Hot or Cold?

Spicy or Sweet?

Fancy or Casual?

Fizzy or Flat?

Stay In or Go Out?

Drink & Sketch

Create a Masterpiece of Drinks...

Create a communal art piece using the blank canvas on the next page.

Sketch your favorite drink or invent a new one with a unique name.

Sign your work of art and invite others to add to the masterpiece.

Your blank canvas awaits...

Create a Signature Sip

Select from each column to craft a cocktail matching your current mood. Visit www.buymeadrink.co/mixieai to discover your drink!

Pick a Vibe	Pick a Twist	Pick a Base
Sunset	Twisted	Mojito
Midnight	Fiery	Margarita
Tropical	Wild	Spritz
Mystic	Frozen	Martini
Velvet	Blissful	Daiquiri
Golden	Sweet	Mule
Moonlight	Sparkling	Colada
Enchanted	Smoky	Punch

Scene & Sidekick

Who comes to mind when celebrating the good times,
giving thanks, or sharing joy?

Cheers-worthy Cocktail
with your BFF who always has your back.

Morning Espresso Shot
with a friend who pushes & inspires you.

Celebratory Glass of Wine
with someone who crushed their goal.

Chai Tea Latte Meet-up
with your favorite creative collaborator.

Craft Beer Cheers
with a bud who knows every local brewery.

Find Your Cheers

Take the quiz to find your ultimate cheers scenario.

What's your ideal weekend?

A. Outdoor adventure: hiking, exploring.
B. City: shopping, museums, restaurants.
C. Relaxing at home: enjoyable book, movies.
D. Socializing: game night with friends.

Pick your favorite vacation spot.

A. Mountain cabin: nature and crisp air.
B. Europe: culture, art, and history.
C. Topical island: lounging on the beach.
D. Wine country: wine tasting and picturesque.

How do you like to unwind?

A. Outdoors: sunset walk or morning jog.
B. Night out: dinner and drinks with friends.
C. Cozy ritual: hot bath, music, and candles.
D. Good company: laughs with friends.

Your Perfect Cheers Is...

Mostly A: Cheers in the Great Outdoors

In a cozy mountain cabin, you and your adventurous best friend toast craft beers by a fire under a starry sky.

Mostly B: City Celebration

At a rooftop bar in New York, you and your friends celebrate the day with a classic martini and skyline views.

Mostly C: Island Chill Cheers

In Hawaii at sunset, you're with your favorite person, sipping Mai Tais and sharing stories as waves crash.

Mostly D: Vineyard Vibes

In Napa Valley, you're touring a winery with a fun group, raising glasses of sparkling wine to living in the moment.

Find Your Path to a Happy Life (or just a Happy Hour)

Paint Your Next Adventure

Get ready to dream big! Here are 5 questions to help you envision the life you truly desire:

What are your top 3 travel destinations, and why?

Who or what inspires you the most in life?

What does your ideal day look like?

What is an experience you crave?

What are 3 things you're a rock star at?

Create the Life You Love

Play Love Hate

In *Love Hate*, you must declare if you love something or hate something - there's no middle ground.

But hey, don't take it too seriously!

Think of "hate" as the playful, exaggerated version of "nah, not for me," and let the game roll....

Love or Hate?

You're asked to give a spontaneous speech at a birthday party.

Sharing food at a restaurant.

Striking up a conversation with a stranger on a plane.

Someone brings a karaoke machine to a dinner party.

You get a surprise birthday serenade at a crowded restaurant.

Getting dressed up to go out for the evening.

Sometimes life's best moments...

Mix & Match

Create your perfect juxtaposition for a fun night in or out. Fancy and casual? Classic and adventurous? Anything goes!

These scenarios are here to inspire your own perfect, quirky combo.

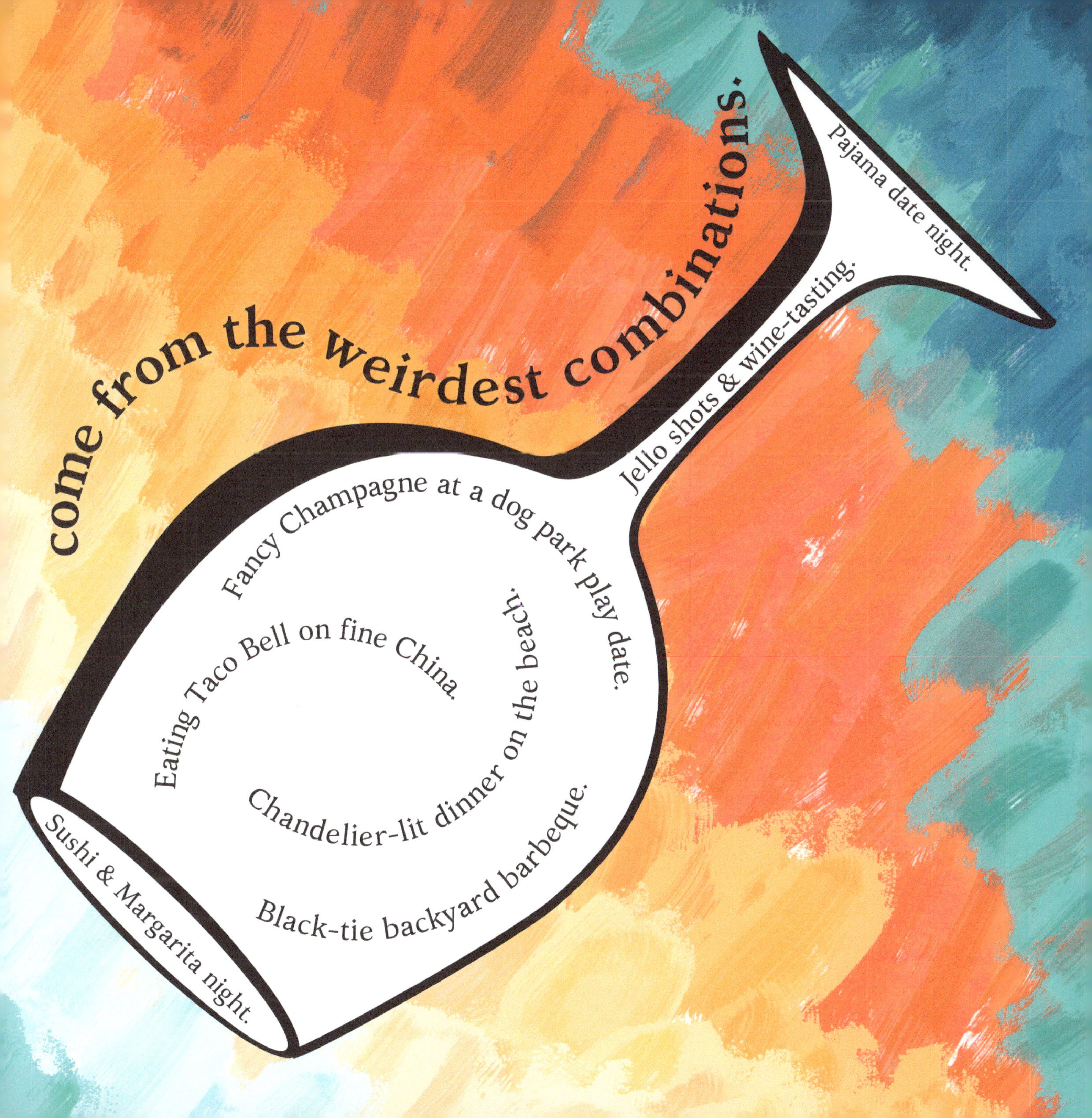

come from the weirdest combinations.

Pajama date night.

Jello shots & wine-tasting.

Fancy Champagne at a dog park play date.

Eating Taco Bell on fine China.

Chandelier-lit dinner on the beach.

Black-tie backyard barbeque.

Sushi & Margarita night.

Sip & Story

Every favorite drink has a story.
What's yours?

Sip & Story

Every sip has a story, and every toast holds a memory. Let's celebrate cheers-worthy moments that make us happy.

We invite you to share a *Sip & Story* with us! Whether it's your go-to cocktail or a time that made you smile, we'd love to hear it.

Head to **buymeadrink.co/sipstory** and share your favorite "cheers" memory.

Moments Worth Spilling...

I had the perfect **mojito**, sunset on **Miami Beach** on my birthday. It wasn't just the drink—it was the breeze and great company!
- Lola

Taking my first sip of the **Cucumber Spicy Margarita** at **Limone's in Asheville** felt like a bust of energy - refreshing, vibrant, and just the right kick of spice. It's now the first place I take out-of-town friends for a "cheers" to welcome them to my favorite city!
- Jillian

Nothing like a delicious **cold light hoppy beer** after a long day while sitting in a **beer garden** and enjoying the company of whoever you're with no matter how ridiculous they are.
- Mark

My first trip to **Maui**, sitting poolside with a **Piña Colada** just taking it all in. I was there with my BF (now husband). It was such a fun, relaxing, adventurous, amazing trip.
- Sara

Another Round...

Life is chaotic and often we need an escape from reality. A bright **Aperol Spritz** is the right balance of dry prosecco and bitter undertones to relax. Perfect when I want to be **swept away** to a nice city moment, a coastal vibe, or my Italian roots.

- Kelly

I always love a **gin & tonic**. The best one I had was in **London**. I was with a group of friends, and we were crying laughing about embarrassing, yet unforgettable moments.

- Jordan

Nothing beats a warm night in **Montana**, sipping **Tequila** and watching the stars roll in. Just you, the breeze, and a little bit of peace.

- Jack

My morning **coffee** dates with my office bestie - couldn't get through the day without them.

- Ren

Last Call...

Celebrating with **Champagne** after purchasing my first home. Yay!
- Carley

Pouring rain, an intimate bar, and a delicious **Espresso Martini** with a good friend. We were at **Lulu's in Delray Beach**—just laughing, brunching, and enjoying the moment.
- Janelle

On a snowy day, my friend and I kicking back with a bottle of **Chardonnay** and a big plate of fries (perfect combo) at our cozy spot by the fireplace at **RL in Chicago**.
- Claudia

We had dinner paired with a **Tequila tasting** in **Cabo**. For each course, we took turns making a silly toast. Good times!
- Brian

Goodbye for Now

Thank you for reading *Hello, Cheers!*
I hope it brought a little joy to your day.

I wanted this book to be a reminder to keep things light, have fun, and celebrate the little wins along the way. Whether it's with a drink in hand or just taking a moment to appreciate the people around us, those small moments matter.

So, let's keep raising a glass to the good stuff—laugh often, live in the moment, and keep creating the life you love.

Cheers to you, and all the moments yet to come!

xo,
Jill

Keep shaking things up.

Let's stay connected!
www.buymeadrink.co

Leo says "cheers" to all the dog lovers out there.

www.ingramcontent.com/pod-product-compliance
Ingram Content Group UK Ltd.
Pitfield, Milton Keynes, MK11 3LW, UK
UKHW061033310726
14089UKWH00010B/221
* 9 7 9 8 3 3 0 4 8 8 6 2 9 *